Volume 87 of the
Yale Series of Younger Poets

NICHOLAS SAMARAS

Hands of the Saddlemaker

Foreword by James Dickey

Yale University Press   *New Haven and London*

Publication of this volume was made possible by a grant from the
Guinzburg Fund.

Designed by James J. Johnson. Set in Garamond type by Tseng Information
Systems, Durham, North Carolina. Printed in the United States of America by
Thomson-Shore, Dexter, Michigan.

Library of Congress Cataloging-in-Publication Data

Samaras, Nicholas, 1954–
    Hands of the saddlemaker / Nicholas Samaras ; foreword by James Dickey.
        p.   cm.—(Yale series of younger poets ; v. 87)
    ISBN 0-300-05457-2 (cloth).—ISBN 0-300-05458-0 (paper)

    I. Title. II. Series.
PS3569.A46295H36   1992
811'.54—dc20   91-31587

10   9   8   7   6   5   4   3   2   1

For, and because of,

Kallistos George Samaras,

my father

And in memory of

Elaine Christine Raftell (1957–1976) and

Linda Raftell (1960–1980)

Contents

Foreword

Nicholas Samaras casts himself, by necessity, chance, and choice, as one of the world's "citizens of transience," always moving, traveling, and yet rooted as well: double-rooted, an American— which, in his case, is to be of both American and European heritages—looking in both homelands, and in many other places, for "the land beyond language."

And yet he is very much *in* language, an early master of strange, honest, and astonishing metaphor, and is a man of feeling, of very strong, almost superhumanly strong, emotion, but in this fact very human, too, as he calls us to follow, to feel more, to *be* more, to encompass and revitalize the earth by means of words and sensibility, no matter where the soul happens to find itself.

Very much a writer of our time, Samaras has, like no one except possibly Graham Greene, the sense of frontiers, of moving from one rooted community to another, into a way of life utterly unlike the one he has just left; belonging, not-belonging, always brooding, wondering, and passing on. The most engaging quality of his work is his metaphysical internationalism, the note of the eternal exile who finds remarkable and life-enhancing particularities in the countries and peoples through which he passes. He knows what is involved when one traverses any of the national shadow-lines and that there, at the border, "It is always three A.M." Moving with him, we see that likewise for us most of these are replaced, they do not exist, they are where we are. We "enter the new country, fresh, chilled, farthingless."

Most of Europe is in Nicholas Samaras's wandering, and—perhaps in the end more foreign—New York, Boston, and California: "Only the Pacific is / wild with personality."

"And all of it new!" New, even—no, especially—awakening in a hospital ward and seeing that your father is standing above your bed.

Samaras's father is a Greek Orthodox priest. To the poet this means churches. Nicholas Samaras understands from a completely individual viewpoint what the connection is between eternal things and the passing world. In his remarkable "In the Shell of a City Cathedral," the poet and his friend Svetozar, a "half-immigrant" he barely knows, determine to enter a cathedral in New York that has been condemned and will be leveled "for further development." Samaras tells us:

Svetozar turns to me, his face urgent. *They're tearing
down this cathedral. We've got to get inside.*

I look at him for the first real time.
We have got to get inside.

Urgent, indeed. The reader is not only caught up in a rare and necessary adventure but is likely to recall how dangerous and precarious it is to enter *any* church, no matter what time of day or night: that the feeling of transgression is part of the pilgrimage. One is reminded of the motion, in James Agee's *The Morning Watch,* when the twelve-year-old protagonist goes into the rural church on Good Friday morning: "To cross its axis without the habitual genuflection felt as uneasy as to swim across a sudden unimaginable depth." Once inside, by an extraordinary sleight of imagination Samaras evokes the bombing of the churches of Dresden and London in so powerful a way that after the journey into the doomed church, the reader, who has followed every forbidden and compulsive step with the poet and his friend—Svetozar with a nail through his foot—has drawn every breath with them, emerges into the early-morning concrete-glass-chromium light of an ordinary city, and feels walking with him the full spread, weight, and depth of religion, knowing with all history-heavy twentieth-century Christians "our eyes hold / the shells of city cathedrals."

This is an extraordinary concept, and once the church has been left and the city re-experienced and deepened by means of it, one holds for a moment stock-still, before moving on to Samaras's most effective and chance-taking contrast, which is between the city church and the wilderness, wherever it may be found. The poet not only enters condemned cathedrals at deadfall of New York night but, crossing borders, with much courage and a highly individual, effortless grasp of metaphor, moves into the wilds and a confrontation with the living and inhuman. He hunts God in the crumbling cathedral but also goes after the wild hog, which can tear his leg off, beyond any religion. Samaras's "Tracking the Boars" is, in its emphatic connection between natural necessity, impulse, danger, and sacrament, enough to give rise to a new term, perhaps *ecclesiastical hunting*.

To sum up, this is the product of a wild and integrated personality, one which is so committed to its subjects that at his best Samaras seems to speak with the voice of an inspired peasant, one who believes in God with his very bone marrow, no matter how much this bewilders him, hour after hour, day after day, place after place. Wherever he finds himself, wherever he wakes or risks his life, he will say what he can, what he has to. Language at its most intense stretch is natural to him and will not be denied. His poems are unique in their orientation and display a linguistics sense that will earn him a wide and discriminating audience.

Speaking for myself but borrowing some of Samaras's words, I go on record here. I buy this view.

James Dickey

Acknowledgments

Acknowledgment is made to the following journals and anthologies for poems that originally appeared in them:

The Albany Review: "Spraying the Bees"
Billie Murray Denny Awards Anthology, 1990: "Easter in the Cancer Ward"
Green Mountains Review: "What Grandfathers Leave"
New Voices, 1979–1983 (Academy of American Poets Awards Five-Year Anthology): "Tracking the Boars"
The New Yorker: "Tracking the Boars"
Open Places: "The Road of One Thousand Trees," "Aubade: Macedonia"
Poetry: "Amnesiac," "Translation"
Poets On: "What Continues"
Wildlife Requiem, by James Balog (New York: International Center of Photography, 1984): excerpt from "Tracking the Boars"

For their valued wisdom, criticism, and guidance, grateful appreciation is expressed to the following persons and organizations: His Eminence, Archbishop Iakovos of North and South America and the Taylor Foundation for study abroad; poetry fellowships from the Aspen Writers Conference, Breadloaf Writers Conference, the National Arts Club, and the New York Foundation for the Arts; Carolyn Forché, Daniel Halpern, Stanley Kunitz, Donald Revell, Daniel Simko, and James Tate.

And for Joan Anderson Mitchell, who taught me the colors of words.

Hands of the Saddlemaker

Παποῦτσι 'απ'τόν τόπον σον, 'ας εἶν'καί μπαλωμένο
A shoe from your own place, even if it is patched

I Citizens of Transience

Lost

The one thing warned against
we have accomplished with remarkable ease.
The path dissolves to darkness.
The forest thickens with night as we fumble
with sweat-dampened matches to set a fire.
On the mountain-slope, wolves chuck their moon-song.
Wild boars rummage the underbrush.
They are far enough away for us to breathe.

I watch while Nikita sleeps, shudders awake
to a blind hour. Embers glimmer a dull red.
Our clothes are limp with smoke
and we prop a paper icon against a tree stump,
chant an ancient tongue to God, tell ourselves
this is the way of all pilgrims.
But oh, how our arms ache
from holding the carvings of our own ribs.

Passport

We arrive when the sky is starless,
leave the car and walk over the bridge,
crossing the dark fleeing river below.
Sentries meet us halfway like an exchange.
It is always three A.M. at the border,
the artificial yellow light harsh on their
uniform buttons and carbines, our pale winter
breaths losing the shapes of our bodies.

These are my papers. Trust me. The photograph
is me, though from a younger lifetime.
This is my longest, warmest coat. It is what I have.
My relation with the person next to me has nothing
to do with the contents of my bags. I claim

no nationality. I am this body
that moves through similar geographies from
sovereign side to sovereign side.
I cannot help but be a citizen of transience,
always looking for the land beyond language.

They escort me to a van and close the curtains,
open the scuffed suitcase, open the toothpaste,
smell the bottled water from Jordan,
stand me up to undress.
These adolescents believe their post is important.
They are bribed by their own lessons of duty
and don't consider what it is they protect.
But I will not recognize it. I want to tell them,

Take the suitcase. It was my father's.
In countries of the temporary, we are forever
accumulating, possessing, leaving behind.   5
In the end, our hands will be finally empty.
Here is the gate your government wrought.
Leaving behind the blunt, obdurate coins
that fall useless between night-borders,
stubbornly ourselves to a state of undress,
we transfer what is transferable, enter
the new country chilled, fresh, farthingless.

Amnesiac

No, I do not remember the rogue car
or how it rode its black metal

6   to the last flash of my bones.
I know only what I've woken to:
two friends bandaged, a bearded man who says he's my father.
The language on my tongue seems thick and faraway.
There is no knife for this illness,
I am a wraith in a white shift.
These are my starched legs, my hands.
This is the mirror that opens on absence.

I accept shadows in my mind.
My father's thinned lips are not mine.
Fear is a comparison and I have
no past to hold it up against.
The neurosurgeon frowns leaving the room. I stare
at the strange flowers breathing my air. The air singes me.
And all of it new! All of it, a face emptied.
I have told my told story
to the statisticians, my history
married to a white bracelet on my wrist.

Women in coarse sheaves of white
glide in to anoint: a gauzy touch
to tighten the dripping I.V.
Salved for consecration, I could
stay this pure
yet fidget for something to happen.
My father moves his lips.
Shadows wash the room, darken his features.
The room breathes in when I breathe in.
The flowers clot in their vase.

This bed drains me,
it draws like a poultice.
Yet the mirror alarms me most.
Three days of light bloomed and wilted on the wall
before they allowed one in.
Nothing there.
The world is a shock. I make a bargain with God.
My hands, untied, feel the folds of my face.
The fugue-probe hurts my brain. My hands
give up, smooth over sterile sheets, settle on nothing.

In the Shell of a City Cathedral

You and I are of uncertain histories.

Listen. We have moved into this story without reason.
There is only the same darkness

numbing the New York buildings in dusky silhouettes
and anonymity. At such midnights, on such streets,

my eyes have always hurried ahead, my footsteps anxious
for a lobby's light. But this night is not done with us,

and Svetozar is suddenly agitated, paces, stops.
He breathes as though he's been gut-punched, makes me

look up. The brownstone rides into deep shadow,
scarred with boards, sleeping bodies along its alcoves.

Svetozar turns to me, his face urgent. *They're tearing
down this cathedral. We've got to get inside.*

I look at him for the first real time.
We have got to get inside.

What is it that turns, at times, in each of us?
I cannot see a name, a christening, a hinge on this church.

Yet I know there are reasons for actions, reasons
beyond verbalizing. Some things are crazy.

I see it is important to him,
this friend I know truly little about, but often think

mad in the finest sense,
both of us half-immigrants,

half-natives to ourselves, both of us
fluent in assimilation. I think of risk, the impracticality

of good clothes. Yet, our lives at rest
have held emptiness in their hands.

Strife has filled them. In this black hour, I think
of every man who has forgotten his fourteenth year

and decide. There is nothing worse than a safe life.
I nod my head, almost smile at the way my body turns

easily to the narthex, the boarded archway, how we
hunch our shoulders together, pry the plywood off

and squeeze ourselves in.
Darkly, we enter the husk of our time.

I am blind and cannot move.
Svetozar is a black shape next to me, breathing in the dry smell.

Slowly, our new world adjusts.
Dull shards of moonlight filter in.

Men whisper in the face of holiness, or terror.
I see to the nave a long floor of wreckage, tendrils of wires

from walls, dark tubings like anacondas, the twisted filigree.
Mindless wreckage, the holy and the profane strewn at my feet.

Above us, a staircase descending into air, black-pocked space.
A banister with missing rungs, the ornate spindling

of the wicks. Beyond that, the disembodied choir-loft,
the hellish chorus. Mindless. The sight exhausts me.

Svetozar swears in as many languages as he knows,
stares ahead and whispers

to no one:
This was a Church.

There is no question or answer. In this place now,
all words are a curse, or a prayer.

I have always been afraid of the unstable.
How such a building, such solidity

can fall to man's priorities.
When first we met, Svetozar, and you witnessed

my English grammar, my undefined American accent,
my mediterranean laughter, you said,

You and I are of uncertain histories.
Now tonight, amid this—when what was this solid falls,

perhaps all histories are uncertain.
All priorities hold the dry horror of change.

I move forward.
Stepping on razed planks that creak

under my weight, stepping over ruin,
silenced rites, the corpses of Saints,

where is the Altar, the four corners
to secure the world?

There is one way to the fractured staircase. Past
the tiny bulldozer with its hard, sleeping teeth.

A ten-foot climb to the landing. Svetozar clambers
up into shadows, treads heavily. Thick dust spirals

down, motes in moonlight. One quick cry.
He lumbers above me, cradles his foot, pulls

slowly, pulls largeness from himself:
a board, a nail gone dark and wet.

I shove my bag up. He reaches down for my arms.
Hoisting up, a splinter takes half my sleeve,

plucks my forearm and, for a long second,
the skin is white like light.

Breathless, I cannot see his leg
and he whispers, Keep moving.

Skuffing down debris,
coughing through dust,

I go over this city's
progress, the devolution.

Ascending, I can believe I am
shedding time, unraveling myself.

This is not here.
This is Bratislava. The darkness of stones falling.

The air whistling for death,
for boys in shiny buttons who went off to be

so quickly wounded.
This is New York City. This is a picture of Dresden.

It is my beloved Foxton, the Cambridge alcove
against London's Blitz, the bomb shelters blooming with heather.

It is this year ascending to apex.
It is the one enduring war.

Ascending, these are not my footsteps.
Yet, whose body is this climbing?

Whose body is this next to me, limping
upward, balanced precariously against pain?

Far over the apse, the sky opens to us through half a roof.
Our boots scrape away a space to sit. Svetozar leans against

black tile, a cinderblock retaining wall, exhausted,
opens a match and sucks the crippled night and tobacco-smoke

through his teeth. He grimaces with happiness,
exhales the ache of air,

our effort and the dull pain, feeling the heavy
pulsing in his fingertips.

I think of the earlier meal,
the Tibetan cabbage, its hard, little leaves like shrapnel;

think of below, the broken, laid-out vagrants who watched us
warily from their stoops, their cardboard beds.

Above us: a vivid half-moon, the city's rusty glow.
This place, so like tonight,

a tomb for faith.
To the right of us, a blue space for prayer

and a hundred-foot drop.
But the nail through your foot.

This is the price of trespass: to come
down and away different.

Svetozar, I sense this is as far as we may go together.
You hold alone the private holiness of your own folded hands.

In matchlight, we see his foot's dark puncture, the skin
gone shiny and red. Left alone, black lines will ascend

the calf—but he draws on his cigarette, exhales.
Shoe back on, he wobbles upright, helps me up.

In another time, Svetozar, your hands
have worn the dash of gasoline.

The starless nights when tanks rumbled through your home-border
and there could be no sleep.

Your small hands, then, that cradled a thirteen-year-old's chin
and what signs that could be turned,

what could be learned in a night's resistance.
Perhaps, tonight, we've climbed to resist

ourselves in a complacent country. What of our own
histories, shared or alone, is certain?

What choices did we assume slowly, like old clothes that wore
our shoulders, our soft bruises like flannel?

To enter this edifice, this cathedral
was necessary. It was both our choice

and in this we were equal.
In the morning, we may find words for what we

expected, or didn't expect, to find,
why we came in the first place, why then we chose to remain.

We have climbed this far. We have climbed
to sturdy, stained-glass stars, climbed to view the ground.

I have all my life been climbing to such—
a clear height, a level footing, an icon

and a dusty mirror.
All through a palpable darkness, the ginger

feeling for where the foot should go next,
the leaning of my weight into it.

Wind filters through our clothes. For a moment, I thought
I heard the connected lives of others,

human cries, voices
that had traveled far north.

Now, we descend carefully.
In the end, Svetozar, we are earthbound

and resume our bodies.
In the early light, what

can be the same?
For days, I know my hands will not be

my own. They hold now
the weight of the banister, the stubborn, faithful broadbeams.

And our eyes, our eyes hold
the shells of city cathedrals.

The Road of One Thousand Trees

All the stops here have exotic names:
    Saint Pavlos, Three Hours of September . . .
I know no one, grow
invisible in that state.
Each time the language inverts
dyslexic on my tongue, I tell myself
I belong here.

But I lie.
The money is soft, spiral pastels in my hand.
My clothes are obvious to native eyes,
skin too white by their easy browns.
I have yet to learn the major roads,
not stare when men walk arm-in-arm,
their faces smooth.
The bus brakes at Cypress Fire,
trees rise like dark flames.
Bodies stammer on, laugh
with dense conversation.
    Let this year abrogate itself.
Below me, the Aegean harbor swallows the sky
and I am a newcomer in an old house.

My stop of One Thousand Trees.
I wander to my room
with one bed, one chair,
one picture tacked on a wall,
and write to Elaine:
In the streets, other men
look you in the eyes.
    Meet me at Forty Churches.

Spraying the Bees

I bring to this house the rite of possession.

These bees distress me.
They flower the balcony, ferment the air
in a threat I can't live with.

I edge to their hole in crumbled concrete,
hold my breath, spray
and leap back, spray and leap back,
watch as they tumble godless
to hard light,
furrow the air limply
to shake off the chemical pollen.
When their fuzzy bodies are done,
I sweep, spray again, glare
as the last enemies go epileptic, twitch
their plump shells to paralysis.
What nature takes, I take back.

My grandmother would have
loved them for their wax,
squeezed out dark, yellow ribbons,
strung candles to take to the priest
for Vespers.
I saw that art once, in Tripoli,
where the old priest
worked the air with wax,
his long beard swaying,
his fingers staining.

Each day,
I open my windows to a dry breeze,
count the dewed, tiny dead in morning light.

The Persistence of Drones

Warm weather brings them back:
smaller, firmer bodies,
young ones the pesticide missed.

I cannot live with them.
They breathe through their sides.
The membranes of their wings
feather the light from my windows
and I am forced to keep them shut.
They rustle the night
under my floorboards,
fester in my dreams.

Will this go on?
I have measured carefully
this land, my days here
but the construction of this house
betrays me—
I cannot reach the nest-hole's tumor
with my sprays, my potions.
These drones refuse to die.
They recognize the smell of my approach.

They will come again; I know this.
While I sleep, they lie,
scheme a strategy of genes.
Their embryos grow and whiten
like cancerous things.
The pulp of their bodies pumps back,
hardening their colors.
Yellow eyes multiply,
gleam through glazed, waxen sacs.

Easter in the Cancer Ward

Because it has been years since my hands
have dyed an egg or I've remembered
my father with color in his beard,
because my fingers have forgotten
the feel of wax melting on my skin,
the heat of paraffin warping air,
because I prefer to view death politely from afar,
I agree to visit the children's cancer ward.

In her ballet-like butterfly slippers, Elaine pad-pads
down the carpeted hall. I bring the bright bags,
press down packets of powdered dye, repress my slight unease.
She sweeps her hair from her volunteer's badge, leaves
behind her own residents' ward for a few hours' release.
The new wing's doors glide open onto great light. Everything is
vibrant and clattered with color. Racing
up, children converge, their green voices rising.

What does one do with the embarrassment of staring
at sickness? Suddenly, I don't know where to place
my hands. Children with radiant faces
reach out thinly, clamor for the expected bags, lead
us to the Nurses' kitchen. Elaine introduces me and reads
out a litany of names. Some of the youngest wear
old expressions. The bald little boy loves Elaine's long mane of hair
and holds the healthy thickness to his face, hearing

her laugh as she pulls him close. "I'm dying,"
he says, and Elaine tells him she is, too: too
much iron silting her veins. I can never accept that truth
yet, in five months, she'll slip away in a September
night—leaving her parents and me to bow our heads, bury her
in a white wedding gown, our people's custom.
But right now, I don't know this. Right now, we are young,
still immortal, and the kids fidget, crying

out for their eggs. Elaine divides them into teams;
I lay out the tools for the operation.
I tell them all how painting Easter eggs used to be done
in the Old Country. Before easy dyes were common,
villagers boiled onion peels, ladled eggs
into pots so the shells wouldn't break.
They'd scoop them out, flushed a brownish-
red, and the elders would polish and polish

them with olive oil, singing hymns for the Holy Thursday hours.
The children laugh and boo when I try to sing. The boys swirl
speckles of color into hot water, while the girls
time the eggs. When a white-faced boy asks from nowhere
if I believe in Christ and living forever,
I stop stirring the mix, answer, "Yes, I do." I answer slowly
and when I speak, my own voice deafens me.
The simple truth blooms like these painted flowers

riding up the bright kitchen walls. I come
to belief. I know that much. Still, what a man may
do with belief demands more than what he says.
Now, the hot waters are stained a rich red. The eggs have
boiled and cooled. To each set of hands, Elaine gives
one towel, three eggs. I pass the pot of melted paraffin,
show these children how to take the eggs and dip them in
and out. While the wax hardens to an opaque film, we hum

Christos Aneste and the room bustles, ajabber
with speech. Holding pins firmly, we scratch out mad
designs where the color will fill. Small, flurried hands
etch and scrim the shells. Everyone's fingers whorl
and scratch in names, delicate and final.
Edging the hall's threshold, an April's allow-
ance of sun filters through tinted windows. Faces furrow
in solemn concentration. Looking to Elaine, my thoughts clamor

for what is redemptive in illness, for having
a Credo to hold these people to me. Etchings
done, everyone immerses the waxy eggs in the pooled
dye. We *ooh* together when transfigured eggs are spooned
out, wiped, and dried on the counters. Soft wax
is peeled gingerly, flecked away; more *oohs* for the tracks
of limned lines, testimonial names.
We burnish the shells with olive oil for a fine sheen.

For a moment, the cultivated, finished eggs hush
the room. Then, every child goes wild in a rush
to compare, to show the nurses, each
other. The bald boy taps my waist. Lined up and speech-
less, they present me with a bright, autographed
egg, communally done. Elaine makes me close my eyes and laughs
when small limbs push at my back to follow
her. They shove my hands in the cool, wet, red dye. The hollow-

eyed girl squeals till tears streak from her laughing.
Another child cries, "You'll never get it off!"
And today, I don't want to. Today,
we've painted eggs a lively color, not caring
about the body's cells and the cells' incarceration.
I lift my arms to embrace Elaine, dab her nose and chin.
And my hands are vivid red. My hands
are bloody with resurrection

and we are laughing.

Aubade: Macedonia

Χωρίς σύνορα εἴμεθα.
We are without borders.

The airstrip is soggy with humidity.
The dark's edgy light is washed of color:
the sky, the air itself,
glassy-blue, hallucinogenic
over a flat, tufted landscape.
Hellenism has a perfect
adjective for this liquidity,
this glassine quality of my leaving,
my skin sallow with the effort of separation.
            You are silent
as the harbor, brimmed
with alarmingly still blue
water, holds silence.
For our thin time, we lived in one vein.
We were two worlds, converged and tender,
unwilling to answer
a separate continent's call.
All last night, you spoke
in present tenses, spoke
to fill the bedroom's fluent air.
Your mouth darkened with the hours.
We made love fiercely,
            we walked the Macedonian wind.
Faced with distance, we vowed
we'd be inseparable, borderless.
But the single plane before us is real,
tarmac threads down to the mouthing bay,
marram stitches the earth to its end.
Now there is no longer land enough
for what could contain or define us.
            One may leave
but two are left. I board
with hollow, metallic footsteps,
your pleasant scent still on
my hands. My hands

resume their singular shape.
The prop-chug startles the air.

I see you on the runway, framed
by stiffening air, back to the wind,
shaking your cloak of my absence.
We mouth final words, our distinct
worlds resuming perspective.
Your face diminishes in the window.
I am lifted into a borderless horizon
and we are forever
            beautiful, haunting, gone.

In the Wake of Exile

You have been in exile for two weeks.

Boarding the boat that takes you,
you are somewhere far off,
forgetting something,
stitching through a necklace of islands.
It is the journey you make in winter.
The moaning of engines, the heavy
rumble below deck on a black-onyx sea.
You do not eat, and grow invisible.
Stripped of everything,
you sleep like this:
In a berth the size of your body,
your face stubbed into the lumpy pillow,
your left palm cradling
your bruised testicles.
The string of lights fades in the hazy black.
The long beard you said goodbye to.
The long beard you know you are becoming.
The book you translate in your sleep.
On gaunt legs that feel unlike yours,
you leave the cabin and haunt the deck.
Stern-side, the waning moon
puddles in the froth of the wake.
Peer into the darkness.
Write this star down.

A Plum Night in Jerusalem, Three A.M.

Go out into a dry, blue heat.
Walk alone in a sleeping city.

Leave your friend sleeping.
Curve and wind through the old sector.

Come to live only in the oldest sector.
Mark how fine the dust is, how

smooth the cobbled hallways,
how much they are what they are.

Listen to where the report and echo
of your footsteps go, how

many years they travel back.
Know that a city is in its deserted hours.

Know that to be alone is to be for once yourself.
And know there are

stones that breathe.
Stones that remember you,

remember the weight of your stance,
where you've come from and are

going for years.

II Keeping the Flag at Zero

"Not until I sat gazing into the field of green . . . did I ever get the idea of Zero in the heraldic sense. When you spot anything true and clear, you are at Zero.

"What is vital here is land, just land. I had almost forgotten it meant such a simple, eternal thing. One gets twisted, derouted, spavined and indoctrinated shouting 'Land of the Free,' et cetera. Land is something on which to grow crops, build a home, raise cows and sheep. . . . The wine has come. I raise my glass. *Salute . . . and keep the flag at zero!*"

—HENRY MILLER, *The Colossus of Maroussi*

Translation

The rock's grey place is precise
and phrases everything
else.

27

Be ginger.
Sit on the green hill, the high view
sloping in declension.

Watch the movement of trees.
The cursive branches.
Verb of the wind over a whitened plain.

I am home. And lost.
My hands on my knees.
This paper. These words.
Able to look like my father's father, squinting,
I am the hands of the Saddlemaker.

Rising up the olive slope,
the sound
of mule bells tonguing.

On the parchment of land, bodies,
what is rendered
by the creased text in a worker's palms,
the blunt eyes of ancient pictures.

I send this.
Your language
returned to you.

What Grandfathers Leave

Kaparelli, Tripoli, 1979

28

This is the gorse land left me
by my grandfather, the one
I never knew, the one
I learned of from yellowed photographs:
soft moustache, the eyes painted-in,
the one I resented for dying
before I could tell him my name.

Samaras from *Samaria:*
Saddle-maker.
I imagine him under a Peloponnesian sun,
young, soaping the hides
till they bend with a boy's hand,
stain in sepia—
the smell, reassuring as work
in a village with no grades past six—
taking the *inia* in his mouth,
working those straps with his teeth,
learning the trade from his own father.

These were my evening stories:
Ellis Island, the tanneries of Woburn,
a grandparent's slow death in the Choate Memorial
where hushed nurses tended patients
like water over pebbles,
unable to understand the *Theé mou, páre me* . . .

I reach the age of documents,
come back to a place on no map
where old peasants point to a cleft of hills,
a village where the same house stands.
I come from Boston, a stranger
to cracked leathers on the wall,
with familiar cheekbones to call back lineage,
resemblance of a gesture.

Birds I have no names for fold the air.
Theio tethers his braying jenny,
remembers my great-grandfather,
the dark hide of his hands.
His legs are stilted, faster than mine.
My shoes are new.

He laughs at my halting language, hobbles
me to the taverna, tries
to buy me an imported drink.
But he is eighty-three
and the blunt arch of his bones
alarms me.
I can't take his money.
I defer, tell him
next year. Next year,
he says, he'll be dead,
glad to go before his wife
who married him at fourteen.
We drink caramel water—
before the moon rises
to an owl call,
before one's eyes are thumbed shut.

Tonight, he says, he will mark my land
where the olive tree, gnarled as a hand
by labor, uproots to a cloudless sky.
Your hair is the color of smoked hazel, you
have your father's mouth, you are
too polite for a Greek.
He squeezes my wrist under kerosene glow.
Your bones are hard enough to marry.
We can choose a bride tomorrow,
thicken your blood.
Here, they are strong for crops or children.

There is a glimmer of fine earth
in the crease of my palms.
30   I turn them over, finally see
my grandfather in them, in this land.
Fotis, Samariti: I chant the music of my name.
The taverna closes. Crickets scissor the dusk.
We dust ourselves off and hobble home
to a house smelling of bread,
where daguerreotypes hang
in straps of cracked leather, look toward
the sepia slats of the cupboard,
measured by hand, supine.
Each stranger's expression and
cheekbones, a mirror of mine.

What Continues

In this village, old people kiss.
Theio crimps in from the dusk,
switches of hazel in his hands,
says I sleep the wrong hours.
When he turns to the fire,
his bristled cheeks are a glint
of silver, a field-day's face let go.
He coddles his wife in the kitchen,
folds his hands in coarse crinoline
till she pushes him away and he cackles.

The night is a scythe for the light.
The night is a burnt umber.
Theio and I go—
a man's night is spent in the tavern
with its clink of glass on tables.
A woman's night gathers on the door-stoop
as she spins the wool in her hands.
The roles are clear.

We wind back—the important
conversation done—and rake
hazel on the fire.
From the hall, we close the language.
I watch them hobble off together,
holding hands,
shadows deepening their wrinkles.
He is eighty-three, she seventy-nine.
Laid down under the thick wool flokati,

I think of the first night I knocked
on their window-shutters, introduced
myself as their nephew
and they laid their palms on me.
A life away, I think of Elaine
and a song arches in me.
Through the walls, I hear their bed
squeaking an ancient rhythm.

Tracking the Boars

1
You say they are dangerous.

The stout razor of their spines
can come to your waist—
they'll take your leg off
in a stain of red
before you can feel
the shoot of pain, your mouth
open, with no cry.
They go for the goats
when the wind turns rancid.

For this, you will gather the men,
leave the sheep to the women,
the village to the priest.
Not return
till what no one speaks of
is proven.

2
It is a morning wreathed
in the husk of fog.
Plane trees lurch into vagueness.
We meet in the Square, unsheathe
weapons, tighten the girths
of wirehaired mules.

Fotis cradles his World War Two rifle,
taps the casing,
the barrel between his legs,

tells a gap-toothed story
of how his grandfather
was called the Turk-Eater.
        Thano's hair is not yet grey.
Rogue boars have stalked in his sleep
till he woke with the ache
of three toes missing
from a hunt seventeen winters ago.
While dawn burns off the haze,
he loads his pack with wooden darts,
prefers poison to slow the animal.

Though I wear a foreigner's clothes,
I am one of the men,
am herded along.
We split into two parties:
men with Fotis, men with Thano—
the winners take the tusks.
They make me bring my camera
to record the kill.

3
The climb is rough.
The leather of my lungs
dusts in, dusts out.
Gorse bushes rake my legs.
Mule bells are stuffed with rags,
their hooves, muffled with gunnysack.
Strange birds gurgle their calls,
filter the air.

At dusk, we pick up boar-tracks,
hear wind whistle through the foothills.

The village is a wrinkle of white
above the darkening sea.

Our group sets camp, lays stones
to char in a circle.
The copse is a cowl of cottonwood.
The men fog the air with rolled cigarettes,
swill Retsina, the burn
of resin on their tongues.
They cackle their stories,
spit into the fire.
I lie back
and listen to the night hiss.

4
The bleach of dawn.
Three shots—
Fotis can tell how far off
by the length of the echo.
He sniffs the wind, curses
our slow luck.
We saddle.

5
We have the boar's bridle-path,
leave the mules,
climb to its territory.
I stop, suck air
through my teeth.
The wind bruises my lips.

Fotis finds a carved dart
in a knotted tree.

The poison is fresh, one day.

6

Each man is a trigger, a hair stiffened.
Words are left at the campsite.
I had wanted to say something
of ourselves that survives
all this
but knew better, kept quiet.

Wild boars know only
the language of blood.
A boar utters a guttural tongue,
not unlike German;
when we hear it, we will know
a sudden dryness in our throats,
a dryness the women of Ublesk knew
who carried their babies
through a smoky night on fire,
stuffing their mouths with rags
to stop the wailing.

Today, our role plays itself.
I hear a rummage of underbrush.
What will we do when we face it,
the boar's demonic eyes on our barrels,
its nostrils, flared
with the scent of our fear?

7
It is monstrous, half the size of Fotis,
bristling its black,
its hocks taut.
Thano breaks through the brush
and the boar whirls in a grunted, cloven frenzy.
We are all cornered.
Something stirs in me
and I am caught up.
Fotis pushes me back—his eyes
gone wild, gone hungry—
fills the air
with blue smoke and thunder.

Three miles below us,
hooved kids bleat for their mamas.

8
The sky clears.
It is the color
of a mother's vein
that runs down into
the neck of her dress.

My face is rough
with two days' growth,
a small calendar.
The mules drag the huge carcass,
it boar-snout, drying;
the glazed eyes stare at nothing.

Fotis sings an old Resistance song.

9

Air fills with the smell of bread,
the women flutter in windows.
Thano curries the mules
and I do my part:
    focus on Fotis
who strains to lift
the massive boar's black head,
smiles to his men,
the wives,
the butcher in his stained uniform.

It is a hard trophy, the threat of a beast.
We lay the table with linen,
carve the corpse and eat.

Amphilohios

This is the first thing you think of.
It may be the way he fills the room,
how morning light seems to flow over him
and is absorbed into his black cassock.
Immediately, this man, his
long, thick salt-and-pepper beard,
will cause you to think of little else,
will have you realize your future
is never yours
but a wind you may
only tack against.

Because you have never felt anything as
love without possession,
you could think he will want
something, eventually.
You think of everyone
who has ever wanted of you,
think of yourself
who has wanted of your life the most.
But he is simple in greeting,
muslin arms outstretched, shaking
the light from his body.

For three days, he will love you and ignore you—
something you find both appreciated and disappointing.
It is strange how you almost miss the judgment.
Into evening, he sits at a carved
table and studies; you sit
opposite, writing cards or gazing past the balcony,
learning how not to start a conversation.
Looking out to a blue vestment of sky,

you think a benign love is possible.
The weekend visit becomes an icon
40   burning into your sleep.

Before you are ready to give
this up, through a blue-veined wind,
the long boat at midnight leads
its ghostly wake into the harbor,
its fogbell calling.
At the wharf, you look out over the black-robed water.
Father holds you in the lightest way
goodbye, kisses your cheeks, his neutral
beard brushing you like air.
And you love the way you are
lost in the openness of his face. You love
the way you are lost.

For George While Sleeping

(died in the War from sunstroke)

Though you buckled over, frail
with startled moon-eyes, flecks of thin shale,
I can still feel your deep fever   41
blistering up to me from your
aged, ashen sleep. Still the seasons turn
in your yellowed history. August burns
the copper of your hair, boy
doughboy, while your thoughts implore
your wife, teenaged
and waiting. Tempered, you come of age.
Your reddened eyelids close. To the world,
George, bowed and humble, you furl
your arms in answer. Now
I visit your brass-plated name, bringing a widow
friend left waiting. For this, I lay iris
and clove. For this.
O George, grown weary with the world's war,
I bring memory and slight breeze to lay back your fever
blessed. O George Perros, frail under the olive tree,
sleeping warm under the warring marker marked victory.

The Last Weekend in May

Does it matter that it was the last year of the Fifties?
That each boy fought to be the one
to balance the big flag in his belt?
That I, too, on that day in that young year,
wore a scout's blue-and-yellow uniform,
believing what uniforms dress?

In the middle of my life, I close my eyes
and still see those legions of greyed men
with gold buttons stretched over their bellies,
putting on splendid identities
apart from their jobs
in the ordinary schoolhouse,
in the grocery store,
my neighbors marching down the central street
in the brilliant, yellow day.
Between the forest of legs,
I banged ahead of the parade
to lead the excitement,
to share something manly with the men,
to run in and out of the colors
and the camaraderie and the noise
that is both a boy's world
and his training.

The year doesn't matter.
It is still exactly this today.
We love to march for the dead.

Does it matter that it was New York
and almost summer?
It must still be exactly that
on every boulevard every year
with new boys to wave the paper flags
into a blur of celebration
until the white stars collide,
to litter the air with learned patriotism.

It is the year to wake up.
On each last weekend in May,
men gather to what they honor
and no one tells us
there is a certain death that does not lie in the ground.

A child's father who is stone
is a living damage.
A child playing soldier
stalks us.

Let the fashion and adrenaline fade.
History itself tells us history is selective.
Silence tells the obscenity
in the act of a parade.

Raise a flag
the color of absence.
Remember the anniversaries
in humble disgrace.
We must walk through the day in whispers,

44

wear only black in the stone orchard
of the deceased and the quiet
who cannot answer back,
teach our children
the shame of participation
as they touch
the etched granite, the chiseled dates.
The braille of silence informs us.
Let the child in each of us,
grown or stunted,
kneel and stain our knees and listen
to the hard, stone tongues that say,
What lie here are the bones of collusion
that you cannot
commemorate or extol.
In silence, burn
every flag that separates
one soul from one soul.

III Settling Estates

Returning to Stoneham, Massachusetts

Here, the road turns as usual, in half-aware memory. Return
to a place of growing up, after a thousand miles and lives,
and the way is still recognized. My wheels follow the spur
of the road, the name of which I never knew. The hives
of new buildings recede in the rear window. The autumns burn
back, as I turn past the magnolia you kissed me first under. We all drive
by recognition. Past your house, I stop on Montvale Avenue, climb
from the car and walk into the field that took you. Amour.
Hello again. What did we grow to in the grey shawl of time?
Though you were mine, you were God's more.
In the face of that fire, what am I to you now? Without you, I'm
the one who reluctantly became a man, who greys now and prays
for you in a dark room, my prayers, the pressed light under the door.
I am the willow that rises green but leans back to you always,
trunk thickening with age. Separate and together, we come home.
You are bright yellow tulips leaning on a white tombstone.

Chanters

They have returned to each other by accident.

The younger, back in the new part of the world, looks behind in mid-step on the Cathedral stairs, chills to the sight of his elder below him—once someone more than a teacher. His lips thin tightly.

For one long second, the elder's surprise electrifies the air. He reads *bastard* in the younger's eyes as an old scene parries between them. Carefully embracing, they enter through heavy doors to join the priests behind the altar.

The summer light betrays the evening's hour.

They dress their polite banter in black robes. Vespers begins as they step out to the Psaltiri to chant. Together again, the younger leads the elder in harmony; lifts his finger a half-step to keep the elder on line and, though they do not look directly at each other, their voices merge as one, entwining emotions in baritone beauty, another scene between them, reluctant and forever. Now they harmonize. Passionate enemies.

"Forgive the living and the dead."

Saint Kosmas Aitolos

This is the weight of the unresolved dead.

Deep hours. A wooded house
with one yellow pane of light.
Words on a page.
Wind in the foothills.
Years I have carried you like a tombstone in my heart.

Tonight, with this book before me
in simple lamplight,
I find the small surprise of perspective,
feel how one found passage may show
the thin, bright plume beneath a closed door.
            I know you are alive somewhere—
dreaming I hand you a plate of oranges,
each day waking to forget my name,
dressing and arranging your hair
to meet someone younger than I.
Before a stoked spine of fire
with this volume on my lap,
I sit up in the hushed parlor,
remembering the closed history of us,
my old habit of thinking you buried to me.

Now with this quote from a quiet saint,
I care to be winter, choose
to unclasp like leaves.
Hatred has kept me
tied to you, kept me your servant.
Anger is a hard strength that isn't good enough anymore.
So, to this paragraph, I speak your name.
Once.
Simply.

I tell you it is alright.
I let the past be finally adequate.
50   I forgive the living and the dead.
Whichever you are is your own choice.
Mine is to move from this.

Decade

1978

Far coast.
Cragline of Requa, California.
A crescent cove of no mail, no address.

I am a tribe of one
since being called
worse than divorce.

So, because to begin over
is to be reduced,
I return to a place of childhood.
To find zero.
To become zero,
the base wholeness
and topography of it.

What the mind numbs out, the body senses—

To heal from love takes land.
It takes the American coast at its most raw.

Hating the flat
Atlantic, I come to the
far edge.

Only the Pacific is
wild with personality,
throwing its white mane to the air
and the auburn rocks.

On a beach, there is solitude
in the midst of company.
Clammers shuck downline,
diminish in grey mounds.
From a borrowed house,
I watch the jagged heave of land,
the growth and burnoff
where sun warms the ground.

Wind is blue, glassy, less than transparent.
Each successive day, my legs
mat a place of kneeling.
Skin grows brine-tough and brown.
Rosewood hands grip a boneknife
and gouge your name into wood.
My mind busies with nothing,
says *Foxton, Woburn,*
forgets words for everything.

In cooled salt air, this is my body
that untenses and lets wind enter.
I become a sluice of water.
First season.

On season's hinge, I wake to shawls of fog,
gull-caw and glossy seal barks
in the haze and distance.
Boulders ghost offshore.
One teal-blue torchbeam tunnels
out over the rocky cataracts.

In sulfur-light, I wade
into surf and wash my hair,
let the salt air dry me.

Wind kicks up brown leaves.
Against each breakwater squall,
I retreat to the A-frame,
listen to gusts and rain
beat, cleanse, evaporate.
I lean against
the redwood walls,
learning their sturdiness.

From the threshold, I stare
into ocean and light
until my eyes hold icons.
Until there is nothing of me
but reflection.

Heavy-sweatered on the rockshelf,
between crags and crenellations,
I sit in my place, white
rolled-up salvar trousers,
bare heels cupped by sand.
With a stick, I nudge a nubbed starfish,
one small, orange arm growing back in the shallows.

Birds embroider the sun, they are
weighted brushstrokes.
And I, too, am painted in, growing solid.

Against the sky boiling last hours,
I gather burlwood
the color of oxblood.
Small, round pieces not unlike children's skulls.
Other filigreed, cyrillic stems—
spindle shanks and arms like relics of the Mount.
I build fire to push back the dark,
hold my arms to the warm sleeves of light.

Rockweed chars and crackles in the pyre, curling.
Shirtless, mossy-chested,
I breathe woodsmoke deeply,
breathe and close my eyes on its grey narcotic.
Pray that death will smell like this.
Smell this woolly and sweet.

How one season is mother to the next.
A new moon fattens
and splinters on black water forever.
What I learn: Silence tells most when you are lying.

In fire-glow, I read old letters
and then burn them, burn
their lives away,
read them and feed
page by page to hungry tongues,
my face flickering in their last light,
hugging my knees like repentance,
watching flecks of white ash rise
like terns in flight.

Give it to fire.
Give myself to the translucence of air.
I am smoke on water.

Years slough off.

When they begin to mean nothing,
zero embraces.

54

Old friend and enemy,
you are driftwood, given
to whorled, greying air
and spray of landspit.
Give memory enough time,
even hatred will smooth
to a kind of fondness.

At night, I toss the syllables of your name
to the crackle of wood femurs in fire,
to the brine and backwash
riding in on stark white lace on black.
Your name is the sound
of surf over pebbles.

Soul grown finally small,
pack away clothes for rounded shoulders,
the beads of agate and beachglass.
Leave the house, but leave the door unlocked.
You have come from far
to far.

These are the elements that purge.
Fire. Stone. Salt air.

1987

August's Assumption.

Matins begins in Massachusetts.
There are bell tolls, high and silver,
the closed air trembling with them.

From a far edge, I step through heavy doors,
over a sculpted threshold to light a candle.
I come back because you told me, *Stay away.*
The long carpet hushes my feet.

From one life to one life,
as if viewing other people,
strangers,
I see us fourteen years
younger in this eastern church,
even your own ghostly face smooth.

I remember every secret you ever
whispered to me here.
Not even your eyes looking at me.

For eight years, I have not once
taken a razor to my hair.
I have tied it back.
It is a cord the color of smoked hazel.

For eight years, I gave silence.
Though not one of us may be held accountable
for calling out in sleep.

This is how one person's
action governs another's:

Standing wooden rows behind you.
Unhatted, intoning the language
with everyone else.

I note your long hem,
the sweep of a dark satin tide.

What is the call of reconciliation?

You turn. We mirror each other.
My face does not move, it says nothing.
Yours does not move, I cannot read it.
There are ten winters in our faces.

My hands hold a candle between our bodies.
The lit taper ripples the air with heat.
Between us, everything to be said
is reduced, pared.
Between us, the vapor
spirals where we stand immobile.

Fire. Stone. Air.

Notes

"Easter in the Cancer Ward" and "Returning to Stoneham, Massachusetts," are written for Elaine Raftell.

"Amnesiac" is for the two riders throughout the years, Richard Bletsis and Sam Georgiou, although I won't drive in cars with them again.

59

"In the Shell of a City Cathedral" is written for Daniel Simko.

"Amphilohios" is for the most remarkable, humble man whose black clothes radiate brilliant light: the Reverend Father Amphilohios Tsoukos, met on the island of Patmos, under the shadow of the Cave of the Book of Revelations, and honored and valued in my life.

"For George While Sleeping": In 1943, at age nineteen, George Perros was the first soldier from Woburn, Massachusetts, to die for the sake of war. His death resulted from heatstroke caused by excessive drilling while in basic training, in Texas, Amerika.

"*Forgive the living and the dead.*": Saint Kosmas Aitolos, 1714–1799, came from Aitolia, in western Greece. His recorded prophesies and spiritual treatises are scarce in English.